WEST CENTRAL COOKS

Recipes from
West Central Liberal Synagogue,
London

www.wcls.org.uk

INTRODUCTION

Dear Friends,

This book represents a wonderful amalgam of recipes from the West Central Liberal Synagogue community; they are as diverse and wonderful as the membership of WCLS. Many have been handed down through families and will happily allow you to add your own variations, as these are not the assured exactitudes often found in modern-day volumes. The recipes more represent the old-fashioned handwritten notes and oral traditions of how to cook this or that (memories of childhood and young adulthood flooding back). As such many of the quantities, cooking times and temperatures may need a little adaptation to your personal taste and the nature of your ovens. Use your judgement and enjoy!

Julia Wendon, former Chair

London's West Central Liberal Synagogue was founded in the early 20th century by Lily Montagu, one of the founders of Liberal Judaism. Services are held at 3pm on Saturday, originally for the sake of local garment workers who worked on Saturday mornings. The synagogue has many cooks among its members, whose origins stretch from South Africa to Spain, across Europe and Russia, and from North Africa to Bombay. (The Bené Israel have lived in India for hundreds of years.) This explains a few differences in spelling: some call the rice dish pulao, some pilaf. Many Jewish festivals come with traditional food: latkes for Hanukkah, charoset and matzah for Pesach. Only certain foods are "kosher shel Pesach" (proper for Passover). Throughout the year foods based on milk ("milchedik") and meat ("fleishedik") are kept apart.

CONTENTS
Starred recipes have been used at the synagogue.

SHABBAT AND FESTIVALS
Challah for Sabbath meals and festivals
Challah, Regina's
Charoset for Pesach, Apple*   (with Vegan Kneidlach and Vegan Lasagna)
Haroseth, Date*
Cinnamon Balls for Pesach
Rice Chapatis for Pesach
Salmon Cutlets for Pesach
The Neuberger Cheesecake for Shavuot*
Honey Cake for the New Year*
Honey and Almond Cake for breaking the fast on Yom Kippur
Latkes for Hanukkah
Hanukkah Cookies
Hamantaschen for Purim

BREAD AND BAKING
"Our" Sachertorte
All-Bran Rusks
Aniseed Cookies*
Banana Bread
Easy Bagels
Fruit Ring
Israeli Rich Fruit Cake
Jaffa Orange and Almond Cake
Jerusalem Sponge Cake
Madeira Cake
Moist Lemon Cake*
Oat and Nutty Bread

SOUPS, SALADS AND PICKLES
Carrot Salad*
Overnight Cucumber Pickle
Mixed Bean Salad with Chilli Dressing
Red Salad
Russian Salad
Widely Loved Pea Soup

MAIN DISHES
Cheese Soufflé
Chicken Homer with Spinach Rice
Chicken Pilaf in a Lemon Sauce
Fish Cakes
Fish Stew
Fricassée
Hot and Spicy Chicken
Lamb Shanks
Mushroom Pilaf
Smoked Salmon and Cottage Cheese Torte*
Spanish Omelette

VEGETABLES
Black-Eyed Beans
Cabbage and Caraway Seeds
Coconut Rice
Fruit and Nut Pulao
Green Chutney*
Green Pea Pulao
Red Cabbage
Spinach Rice
Stuffed Aubergine

SWEETS AND DESSERTS
Caramelised Oranges
Carrot Halva*
Chocolate Almond Truffles*
Chocolate Coffee Truffles*
Gooseberry Kuchen
Rote Grütze
Spicy Apples
Stewed Apples
Turinois

SHABBAT AND FESTIVALS

CHALLAH FOR SABBATH MEALS AND FESTIVALS
Blasé Roses

My grandmother's recipe. Makes two large loaves.

900g strong white flour
3 tsp salt
4 tsp caster sugar (optional)
4 tsp quick-acting dried yeast
6 tbsp oil
500ml warm water
4 eggs, beaten
Poppy seeds to decorate

Sift together the flour, salt and sugar (if you are using sugar). Sprinkle over the yeast.

Mix the oil with half of the water and 2 eggs beaten together. The water must be warm – if too hot or too cold then the bread will not rise. Add the rest of the water to the flour, and then the oil and egg mixture.

Mix until dough is formed, then knead until smooth and elastic, using a little extra flour if it seems sticky. Put dough in a greased bowl, cover with a clean dish towel and leave in a warm place for at least two hours.

Knock back the dough by kneading it and then divide it into two. Cut each piece into three and roll the sections into long sausage shapes. Using three strands for each loaf, plait the dough.

Tuck the end of each plait underneath and leave the plaited loaves to rise on an oiled baking sheet for about 30 mins.

Preheat the oven to 220°C/425°F/Gas Mark 7. Brush the loaves with the remaining beaten egg and sprinkle with poppy seeds. Bake for about 35-40 mins. Leave to cool on a wire tray for 5-10 mins. Serve hot or cold with butter.

CHALLAH, REGINA'S

Sweet with raisins or savoury with Mediterranean herbs and spices – everyone's weekend pleasure, and for some a pleasure throughout the week.

550g strong white flour
1-1/2 tbsp dried yeast
2 eggs (and 1 egg yolk)

4 tbsp vegetable oil
4 tbsp sugar
1 tsp salt
250ml water

Rosemary, thyme, coriander, marjoram, sage or oregano, fresh or dried

Take half of the lukewarm water, add the vegetable oil, sugar and salt.

Take the second part of the lukewarm water and stir in the yeast. Let it stand for 5 min, stirring occasionally.

Beat the eggs lightly in a large bowl, add the dissolved yeast and the mixture of water and oil. Add half of the flour and knead well.

Place the dough on a floured surface, add the remaining flour while kneading until dough is smooth. (For the sweet option: knead raisins into the dough. For savoury option: knead spices into the dough.)

Coat a bowl with vegetable oil to keep the dough moist, add the ball of dough and cover the bowl with a towel or clingfilm. Let the dough rise to double volume in a warm place. Brush a baking tray with a film of oil.

Knead the raised dough briefly on a floured working surface. Divide dough into three (or four) equal parts and plait it, with the ends tucked under.

Place on the baking tray, brush with egg yolk, let rise again for 5 min. Bake for about 30 min until doubled in volume and lightly browned.

CHAROSET, APPLE
Issy Benjamin

3 apples, unpeeled but cored and diced
1 cup ground almonds
1 cup ground walnuts or hazelnuts
1/2 cup chopped and pitted dates

1 heaped tsp of ground cinnamon (more to taste if desired)
1 cup sweet red wine or grape juice

Mix all ingredients in blender. If the mixture is too moist, add more ground almonds and/or ground walnuts or hazelnuts until the mixture has the fairly stiff consistency of mortar.

This reminds us of the mortar that made the bricks of slavery. (Be grateful that the Egyptian taskmasters withdrew the straw to make things more difficult for the Israelites.) This should be enough for two Seders – and the balance for Hillel sandwiches (matzos filled or topped with charoset and horseradish) throughout Pesach.

Catering on Pesach for vegan sons is difficult... particularly Ashkenazi style (no rice or pulses). For instance, kneidlach (matzo balls in soup) are particularly difficult to make without eggs and chicken shmaltz (fat). So here I will slip in some extra recipes for vegans.

VEGAN KNEIDLACH
Take equal amounts of matzo meal and pesachdik vegetable shortening. Mix dry until crumbly. Add enough boiling water to melt the shortening and make a stiff mix, the consistency of charoset. Mould into balls and freeze.

Just before serving the vegetable soup, drop the frozen matzo balls into the simmering liquid. The instant before the balls begin to disintegrate you need to serve! (The Ashkenazi way to eat kneidlach is with a sprinkle of cinnamon and sugar.)

8

VEGAN LASAGNA
Place a layer of dampened matzo at the bottom of a roasting pan. On this spread a layer of peeled grilled aubergine, and on top of this place another layer of damp matzo. Over this spread a thick layer of cooked tomato followed by another layer of damp matzo. On this spread a layer of cooked spinach, with another layer of damp matzo above topped of with a sort of (vegan) bechamel made from a mix of soya milk and matzo meal.

HAROSETH, DATE
Sophie Jhirad

In Bené Israel tradition, haroseth is made not only for the Seder but in sufficient quantity for all of Pesach. Spread on matzah, or as a dip for lettuce etc, it is truly wonderful. Some families used it throughout Passover as a sweetener instead of sugar, even in tea and coffee (the latter only made from freshly roasted and ground beans) – don't try that! Usually families made their own, but orders could be placed with synagogues.

This recipe gives the quantity I make, but the method is the same for less or more.

2 lb/1 kg stoned dates (not sugared or with any added preservatives)
Water

Wash dates and put into a large pot with enough water to sit well over the dates. Cover and bring slowly to the boil. Boil for a while, uncovered, skimming the surface as necessary. Reduce the heat and leave to simmer, with the lid on but not quite closed, to allow steam to escape. This quantity will take a couple of hours, but in the early stages you do not need to stand over the pot. Stir occasionally. As the liquid reduces, you will need to stir more often. Add a little more hot water if necessary.

Cooking is done when the dates are reduced to such a mush that you cannot distinguish one from another, and all the water has been absorbed or has steamed off. To check, press the back of a spoon on the surface – if thin liquid seeps into the bowl, some more cooking is needed. When cooked, sieve it, either straight away or after cooling.

I was advised to boil this again after sieving, but found the haroseth spat at me rather energetically, so left off. Unnecessary, anyway, as this haroseth keeps very well without that second boil.

Note: I'm told that, in Israel, some Bené Israel have taken to adding nuts to this haroseth. Ouch!

CINNAMON BALLS
Blasé Roses

My grandmother's recipe. Makes about 30.

350g ground almonds
150g caster sugar
2 tsp ground cinnamon
4 large egg whites
Oil for greasing
Icing sugar for covering

Preheat oven to 180°C/350°F/Gas Mark 4. Grease a large baking sheet with oil. Mix the almonds, sugar and cinnamon together.

In a separate bowl, whisk the egg whites until they begin to stiffen and then fold enough into the almond mixture to make a firm consistency.

Wet your hands in cold water and roll small spoonfuls of the mixture into balls. Place these at intervals on the baking sheet.

Bake for about 15 mins in the centre of the oven. They should be slightly soft inside – too much cooking will make them hard. Slide a palette knife under the balls to release them from the baking sheet.

Leave to cool. Sift a few tablespoons of icing sugar onto a plate or into a bowl. When the cinnamon balls are cold, slide them onto the plate or into the bowl. Shake gently until the balls are completely covered in sugar.

Serve with black coffee or tea.

RICE CHAPATIS
Norah Solomon

For Sephardim, rice is kosher shel Pesach, so these come into their own at the festival. Much lighter than wheat chapatis, they may, though rarely, appear on the table any time during the year.

1 level cupful of rice flour (NOT ground rice), plus extra for dusting

1 cupful of water
A good pinch of salt
A little butter (optional)

Bring the water and salt to the boil, then add the rice flour. Lower the heat to the minimum while mixing thoroughly. When well mixed, take off the heat, cover with a cloth and leave to cool. When cool enough to handle, turn out, bring together and knead to form a smooth dough.

Divide into 8 to 10 pieces, each about the size of a walnut. Roll out each piece to approximately 6in/15cm in diameter – if necessary, dust the board and rolling pin *lightly* with rice flour.

On a moderate flame, heat a dry frying pan, preferably non-stick. Test the temperature by sprinkling a few drops of water on the pan – if the water dries immediately, the pan is ready to receive its first chapati.

Place the chapati on the frying pan. In a little while, steam will rise around the edges. Turn over and cook the underside, moving the chapati gently now and then to prevent it sticking. When the underside is done, turn over. The chapati will begin to puff up. With a cloth crumpled in your hand, press down on the sides, spinning slightly each time.

When cooked – each chapati will take about 2-1/2 mins – place in a flat-bottomed dish lined with a cloth. Fold the cloth over to keep the chapatis warm.

If you wish, spread a tiny dab of butter across each chapati as it comes off the frying pan, and fold in half. But this is gilding the lily.

SALMON CUTLETS
June Levy

1 213g tin of pink salmon
1 213g tin of red salmon
1 small shallot, finely chopped
1/2 a large egg
2 tbsp matzo meal
1 tbsp parsley
Salt and pepper to taste
Oil for frying

Drain the tins of salmon and remove any black skin and bones; crumble until it resembles fine breadcrumbs.

Add shallot, matzo meal, parsley, salt and pepper. Bind together with egg; make into cutlets.

Fry in hot oil. I try it first with a tiny one to see if the mixture is the right consistency – if too wet, add matzo meal; if too dry, add egg.

Should make about nine cutlets.

THE NEUBERGER CHEESECAKE
Julia Neuberger

This has no base, so it needs to be made in a loose-bottomed 8in cake tin with a tray underneath – it drips!!!!

450g (675g if feeling very generous) curd cheese or soft non-fatty cream cheese

225g (450g if feeling very generous) cream cheese, full fat

Approx. 75g caster sugar (You may like more – I don't like things too sweet.)

1 tsp good quality vanilla essence
4 large eggs

For the topping
1 large carton sour cream or creamed smatana if you can get it
1 dessertspoon caster sugar
1 tsp good vanilla essence

Mix all the ingredients for the cake, but not the topping, in a food mixer – not a processor as it gets too grainy – and turn into the cake tin.

Bake at about 150°C/300°F/Gas Mark 2 for 50 mins – it should be browning slightly at the edges. Take out. Turn oven to 220°C/425°F/Mark 7.

Make topping by mixing ingredients and pour over top – it will sink in the middle but *don't worry.* Put back in oven and cook for approx. 10 mins.

Remove from oven and allow to cool completely before putting in fridge. Do not remove from tin until ready to serve.

It's best if served when cool but not refrigerated, the same day as baking it. If you can't serve it the same day, remove from fridge an hour before serving.

HONEY CAKE FOR THE NEW YEAR
Luba Jamieson

Luba contributed this recipe to the Chaverim newsletter well in time for members to make the cake for Rosh Hashanah. She was given it years ago by her hairdresser, whose grandmother's recipe it was. It works beautifully, right down to the cooking time given.

2 standard eggs (take out of fridge into warm room)

100g/4 oz soft dark brown sugar
250g-275g/10oz self-raising flour
1 tsp mixed ground spice (heaped)
1 tsp cinnamon (heaped)

1/2 tsp ground ginger
1 tsp bicarbonate of soda (heaped)
100g/4 oz runny honey
100g/4 oz golden syrup or treacle

3 tbsp oil
150ml/1/4 pint warm water
Flaked almonds for decoration

Heat oven to 190°C/374°F/Gas Mark 5. Beat eggs and sugar together until light and frothy. Beat wet ingredients (honey, syrup/treacle and oil) together. Add to beaten eggs and sugar *quickly* – beat for a couple of minutes. Mix dry ingredients together.

Take your main bowl and add dry ingredients and wet mixture alternately, a little at a time, making sure that ingredients are well mixed before adding more. When smooth, add the warm water and mix well again.

Line baking dish with Bakewell Paper (baking parchment). Pour in mixture and place flaked almonds on top for decoration. Place in ready-heated oven on second shelf for 30 mins. (Do not open oven door during this time.) Then reduce heat to 180°C/350°F/Gas Mark 4 for a further 30 mins, and it should be done – a dark rich brown.

It tastes better as it matures.

HONEY AND ALMOND CAKE
Blasé Roses

My grandmother's recipe for breaking fast on Yom Kippur. Serves 16 people.

150g/5-1/2 oz unsalted butter, plus extra for greasing

150g/5-1/2 oz soft brown sugar
4 large eggs, beaten
350g/12 oz self-raising flour
2 tsp baking powder
8 tbsp milk
4 tbsp honey
100g/3-1/2 oz flaked almonds

For the syrup
450g/8 oz honey
4 tbsp lemon juice

Preheat the oven to 180°C/350°F/Gas Mark 4. Grease and line a 36cm/14in round or square cake tin.

Place the unsalted butter, sugar, eggs, flour, baking powder, milk and honey in a large mixing bowl and beat well with a wooden spoon for one to two minutes, or until all the ingredients are thoroughly mixed together.

Spoon into the prepared tin, smooth the surface with the back of a spoon or a knife, and sprinkle with the flaked almonds.

Bake in the preheated oven for about 50 mins, or until it's well-risen and a skewer inserted into the centre comes out clean.

Meanwhile make the syrup: combine the honey and lemon juice in a small saucepan and simmer over a low heat for about 5 mins, or until the syrup coats the back of a spoon.

As soon as the cake comes out of the oven, pour the syrup over it, allowing it to soak in. Leave the cake to cool in the tin for at least two hours before slicing.

LATKES: QUICK AND SLOW
Julia Wendon

2 lb (1 kg) potatoes
2 large eggs
Salt
Oil for frying
Black pepper, chopped parsley, finely chopped onion (optional)

Peel and finely grate the potatoes. Put them in a colander and rinse under the cold tap. Drain, and squeeze dry in a tea towel.

Beat the eggs lightly with salt, add to the potatoes, and stir well. Heat a little oil in a frying pan. Take serving-spoonfuls, or a 1/4 cup (50 ml), of the mixture and drop into the hot oil. Flatten a little, and lower the heat so that the fritters cook through evenly. When one side is brown, turn over and brown the other.

Lift out and serve hot. Eat immediately!

You can add black pepper, chopped parsley and finely chopped onion to the egg and potato mixture.

Instead of the egg, you can add 4-1/2 tbsp of flour to the mix, or the same quantity of mashed potato. Or, for speed, you can leave out the egg and flour.

HANUKKAH COOKIES
Blasé Roses

My mother's recipe.

1 cup butter
2 large eggs, beaten
2 tsp vanilla
1/2 cup brown sugar
1 cup white sugar
1-1/2 cups flour
1/2 tsp salt
1/2 tsp baking powder
2-1/2 cups semi-sweet chocolate chips

Preheat oven to 190°C. In a small bowl, stir together flour, baking powder and salt. Set the mixture aside.

In a large bowl, cream together the butter and sugar until smooth.

Beat in the eggs and vanilla, gradually blend in the dry ingredients (and chocolate chips).

Roll rounded teaspoonsful of the dough into balls and place onto an ungreased cookie sheet.

Bake 8-10 mins in the preheated oven, or until golden brown.

Let stand on cookie sheet for 2 mins (to hold shape) before removing to cool on wire racks.

HAMANTASCHEN
Blasé Roses

My mother's recipe for Purim. Please note – it always worked better for my mother to cover the dough and refrigerate overnight.

6 large eggs
2 cups granulated sugar
1-1/2 cups olive oil
5 tsp vanilla extract

1 cup orange juice (pure)
11 cups all-purpose flour
2 tsp baking powder
2 cups fruit preserves, any flavour

Preheat oven to 175°C/350°F. Grease cookie sheets.

In a large bowl, beat the eggs and sugar until light and fluffy. Stir in the oil, vanilla and orange juice.

Combine the flour and baking powder, and stir into the batter to form a stiff dough. If the dough is not stiff enough to roll out, stir in more flour.

On a lightly floured surface, roll dough out to 1/4 in thickness. Cut into circles using a cookie cutter or the rim of a glass.

Place cookies 2 in apart on the prepared cookie sheets. Spoon about 2 tsp of preserves into the centre of each one. Pinch the edges to form three corners.

Bake for 12-15 mins in the preheated oven, or until lightly browned. Allow cookies to cool for
1 min on the cookie sheet before removing to wire racks to cool down completely.

BREAD AND BAKING

"OUR" SACHERTORTE
Julia Wendon

200g good quality chocolate
150g butter
6 eggs
180g sugar
150g ground almonds
Vanilla pod or vanilla extract (optional)
Raspberry or apricot jam
Cream for whipping

For coating
100g chocolate
100g butter (or cream)

Melt the chocolate with the butter. (I used to do this over a water bath but I now do it in the microwave.) Separate the eggs. In a separate bowl beat the egg yolks and sugar until pale. Vanilla can be added if desired (one pod or 1/2 tsp of extract).

Mix together the chocolate mixture and the egg/sugar mixture. Beat the egg whites until stiff and fold into the egg and chocolate mixture. Gently fold in the ground almonds.

Pour into two prepared cake tins and cook at 180°C for 30-35 mins. Take out of the tins and cool.

Warm raspberry jam in a small pan (purists may choose apricot). Sandwich together the two cake sections with jam, and also coat the top and sides. Coat with either a ganache of chocolate and butter melted in a microwave, or a 50:50 mix of melted chocolate and cream. Serve with whipped cream.

ALL-BRAN RUSKS
Blasé Roses

My mother's recipe. Makes about 80 large rusks to enjoy with coffee or tea.

8 cups self-raising flour
1-1/2 tsp salt
1 tsp baking powder
6 cups All-Bran Flakes
1-1/2 cups buttermilk
1-1/2 cups sugar
3 extra-large eggs, beaten
500g butter, melted

Preheat oven to 180°C. Butter three 28cm x 11cm loaf trays.

Sift the flour, salt and baking powder together in a large mixing bowl. Add the All Bran Flakes and sugar.

Mix the melted butter, buttermilk and eggs together and add to the dry ingredients. Knead until combined.

Shape the dough into balls and place two balls side by side in rows in the prepared loaf trays.

Bake for 30-45 mins or until a skewer inserted into the centre comes out clean. Turn out onto a wire rack to cool.

Break the rusks apart and cut each in half. Dry out on baking trays at 90°C-100°C for
4-5 hours.

ANISEED COOKIES
Amina Zairi

I have known these North African cookies all my life and, as a child, used to help my grandmother make them for special occasions. With basic ingredients, they are easy to make.

The use of aniseed in cakes was introduced to North Africa by Moriscos from Spain. Makes approx. 40 cookies.

4 tbsp ground aniseed
3 medium eggs
30ml (or one cup) oil
200g (or one cup) sugar

Self-raising flour – enough to make a soft dough
Vanilla essence (liquid – more potent – or powder)

Pre-heat oven to 200°C/392°F/Gas Mark 6.

Beat the eggs very well for a minute or two. Add the oil, continue to beat until egg and oil are well-mixed and smooth.

Add sugar and continue mixing. Add vanilla and aniseed.

Gradually introduce sifted flour into the mix, and continue mixing until a soft dough is achieved.

Roll out dough, cut into shapes, and put these on a flour-dusted baking tray.

Bake in the pre-heated oven for 10 mins, then reduce temperature to 190°C/374°F/Gas Mark 5 for
30 mins – or until golden.

Leave to cool in the tray for half an hour before transferring into a cookie jar.

BANANA BREAD
Blasé Roses

My grandmother's recipe.

250g/8.8 oz butter, unsalted
2 cups sugar
4 large eggs
1 tsp vanilla essence

8 bananas
4 cups flour
1/2 tsp salt

4 tsp Royal baking powder
1/2 tsp bicarbonate of soda
1/2 cup milk
Sultanas (optional)

Cream together the butter and sugar.

Add eggs one at a time and beat each in thoroughly. Add vanilla essence.

Mash bananas well and stir into the mixture. (Add sultanas if using.)

Sift in the flour, salt and baking powder.

Mix bicarbonate of soda with a little milk and add to the mixture. Gradually add the 1/2 cup of milk and beat mixture thoroughly.

Turn into an 18in/46cm x 8in/22cm (approx.) loaf tin and bake for one hour at 180°C.

Serve plain or buttered.

EASY BAGELS
Blasé Roses

My grandmother's recipe. Makes 36.

3 lb strong white flour
4-1/2 tsp salt
3 sachets easy-blend dried yeast (about 21g)
9 large eggs
3 tsp clear honey
6 tsp sunflower oil
600ml tepid water

Preparation: 1 hour 35 mins, cooking 15 mins.

Put the flour into a large bowl and stir in the salt and yeast. Make a well in the centre. Lightly whisk 6 eggs with the honey and oil and pour into the well in the flour. Add the water and mix to a soft dough. Turn out onto a lightly floured surface and knead for 10 mins, or until smooth and elastic. Place the dough in a large greased bowl, cover with a damp tea towel and leave to rise in a warm place for 40 mins or until doubled in size.

Turn out the dough onto the floured work surface and knead it lightly. Divide it into 36 equal pieces, and form each into a 20cm (or 8in) sausage. Shape into a ring, dampen the ends with a little water, slightly overlap them and gently pinch together to seal.

Arrange the bagels on a lightly oiled baking sheet, cover with oiled clingfilm and leave to rise in a warm place for 20 mins or until they are slightly puffy.

Preheat the oven to 200°C/400°F/Gas Mark 6. Bring a large pan of lightly salted water to the boil, drop the bagels into the water one at a time for 20 sec only, lift out with a large draining spoon and return to the baking sheet.

Lightly beat the 3 remaining eggs and brush them over the bagels to glaze. Bake for 14-15 mins or until well risen and golden brown. Transfer to a wire rack to cool. The bagels can be kept in an airtight container – for no longer than three days.

FRUIT RING
Blasé Roses

My grandmother's recipe. Serves 24 people.

Oil or melted butter for greasing
4 tbsp lime juice or lemon juice

200g/7 oz dried tropical fruit, such as mango, papaya and/or pineapple, roughly chopped, plus extra to decorate

350g/12 oz plain flour
5 tsp baking powder
350g/12 oz unsalted butter, softened

350g/12 oz golden caster sugar
6 large eggs, beaten
2 tsp vanilla extract

For the icing
140g/5 oz icing sugar
2 tbsp lime or lemon juice

Preheat the oven to 160°C/325°F/Gas Mark 3. Grease a 3-litre/5-pint ring cake tin, preferably non-stick. Stir the lime or lemon juice into the dried tropical fruit and leave to soak for 15 mins.

Sift the flour and baking powder into a large bowl and add the butter, caster sugar, eggs and vanilla extract. Beat well until the mixture is smooth, then stir in the soaked fruit.

Spoon the mixture into the prepared tin and smooth the surface with a palette knife. Bake in the preheated oven for 40-50 mins or until risen, firm and golden brown. Leave to cool in the tin for 10 mins, then turn out and finish cooling on a wire rack.

For the icing, sift the icing sugar into a bowl, add the lime or lemon juice and stir until smooth. Spoon the icing over the cake and decorate with dried tropical fruit. Leave to set before slicing.

ISRAELI RICH FRUIT CAKE
Blasé Roses

My grandmother's recipe. Serves 32 people.

700g/24 oz sultanas
450g/12 oz raisins
230g/8 oz ready-to-eat dried apricots, chopped
170g/6 oz stoned dates, chopped

Finely grated rind and juice of 2 oranges
Oil or melted butter, for greasing
450g/16 oz unsalted butter
450g/16 oz light muscovado sugar

8 eggs, beaten
140g/5 oz chopped mixed peel
170g/6 oz glacé cherries, quartered
50g/2 oz chopped glacé ginger or stem ginger

80g/3 oz blanched almonds, chopped
400g/14 oz plain flour
2 tsp ground mixed spice

8 tbsp dark rum or brandy, plus for flavouring (optional)

Place the sultanas, raisins, apricots and dates in a large bowl and stir in the rum or brandy, orange rind and orange juice. Cover and leave to soak for several hours or overnight. Preheat oven to 150°C/300°F/Gas Mark 2. Grease a 40cm/16in round deep cake tin and line with baking paper.

Cream together the butter and sugar until light and fluffy. Gradually beat in the eggs, beating hard after each addition.

Stir in the soaked fruits, mixed peel, glacé cherries, glacé ginger and blanched almonds.

Sift together the flour and mixed spice, then fold lightly and evenly into the mixture.

Spoon the mixture into the prepared cake tin and level the surface, making a slight depression in the centre with the back of the spoon.

Bake in the preheated oven for 2-1/4 to 2-3/4 hours, or until the cake is beginning to shrink away from the sides, and a skewer inserted into the centre comes out clean. Cool completely in the tin.

Turn out the cake and remove the lining paper. Wrap in greaseproof paper or foil, and store at least two months before use. To add a richer flavour, pierce the cake with a skewer, and spoon over a couple of extra tablespoons of rum or brandy, if using, before storing.

JAFFA ORANGE AND ALMOND CAKE
Blasé Roses

My grandmother's recipe. Serves 16-20 people.

Oil or melted butter, for greasing
4 large oranges
110g/4 oz ground almonds
230g/8 oz plain flour

2 tsp baking powder
170g/6 oz unsalted butter, softened
350g/12 oz caster sugar
6 large eggs, beaten

2 tsp orange-flower water
4 tbsp orange juice, natural
4 tbsp toasted flaked almonds

Strips of orange zest, to decorate

Wash the oranges and place in a saucepan, then cover with boiling water and simmer for one hour, covered, until soft. Drain and leave to cool slightly. Cut the oranges in half and remove and discard any pips. Purée in a food processor or blender until smooth, then stir in the ground almonds.

Preheat the oven to 160°C/325°F/gas mark 3. Grease and line a 46cm/18in round deep cake tin.

Sift the flour and baking powder into a large bowl and add the butter, sugar, eggs and orange-flower water.

Beat well until the mixture is smooth. Add the orange and almond mixture and the orange juice, mixing evenly.

Spoon the mixture into the prepared tin and smooth the surface with a palette knife. Bake in the preheated oven for 40-50 mins or until the cake is firm and golden brown. Leave to cool in the tin for 2-3 mins, then turn out and serve warm, topped with flaked almonds and strips of orange zest.

JERUSALEM SPONGE CAKE
Blasé Roses

My grandmother's recipe. Serves 16-20 people.

350g/12 oz unsalted butter, softened, plus extra for greasing

350g/12 oz caster sugar
6 large eggs, beaten
350g/12 oz self-raising flour
pinch of salt
6 tbsp strawberry or raspberry jam
2 tbsp icing sugar
2 tbsp brandy

Preheat the oven to 180°C/350°F/Gas Mark 4. Grease and line the base of two 40cm/16in sandwich cake tins.

Cream the butter and caster sugar together in a mixing bowl using a wooden spoon or an electric mixer until the mixture is pale in colour and light and fluffy. Add the eggs a little at a time, beating well after each addition.

Sift the flour and salt into a separate bowl and carefully add to the mixture, folding in with a metal spoon or spatula. Divide the mixture between the prepared tins and smooth over with the spatula.

Place the tins on the same shelf in the centre of the oven and bake for 25-30 mins until the cakes are well-risen, golden brown and beginning to shrink from the sides of the tin.

Leave to cool in the tins for one minute, then turn out onto a wire rack to cool. When completely cool, pour the brandy into the sponge, sandwich together the cakes with the jam, and dust with the icing sugar.

MADEIRA CAKE
Blasé Roses

Jewish style by my grandmother. Serves 16-20 people.

350g/12 oz unsalted butter, plus extra for greasing
350g/12 oz caster sugar
Finely grated rind of two lemons
6 large eggs, beaten

230g/8 oz plain flour
230g/8 oz self-raising flour
4-6 tbsp brandy or milk according to taste
4 slices of citron peel (or zest of a lemon)

Preheat the oven to 160°C/325°F/Gas Mark 3. Grease and line a 36cm/14in round deep cake tin.

Cream together the butter and sugar until pale and fluffy. Add the lemon rind and gradually beat in the eggs.

Sift in the flour and fold in evenly adding enough brandy, or milk, to make a soft dropping consistency.

Spoon the mixture into the prepared tin and smooth the surface. Lay the slices of citron peel on the top of the cake.

Bake in the preheated oven for 1 to 1-1/4 hours, or until well-risen, golden brown and springy to the touch.

Cool in the tin for about 10 mins, then turn out and cool completely on a wire rack.

MOIST LEMON CAKE
Sophie Jhirad

At my last job, when we were going through a slack period, the advertisement manager brought in a load of his wife's magazines for me to read. I skipped through them to pick up anything useful or interesting – of the three recipes garnered this is my favourite. I use a square tin instead of the oblong recommended, and the mixer works much better than any wooden spoon wielded by me.

6 oz/171g self-raising flour
1 level tsp baking powder
Pinch of salt
4 oz/113g soft creaming margarine
4 oz/113g caster sugar

Grated rind of one lemon
2 large eggs
1 oz/28g coarsely chopped walnuts
2 tbsp milk

For the lemon syrup
Juice of one lemon
4 oz/113g icing sugar

Heat oven to 350°F/180°C/Gas Mark 4. Grease an oblong baking tin (11in x 7in x 1in) and line with a strip of greaseproof paper cut the width of the tin and long enough to overlap the opposite ends.

Sift the flour, baking powder and salt into a mixing bowl. Add the margarine, sugar, eggs, lemon rind, walnuts and milk. Using a wooden spoon, stir to blend the ingredients, then beat well for one minute to get a smooth cake batter.

Turn the mixture into the prepared tin and spread level. Set in the centre of the preheated oven and bake for 40 mins.

Make the syrup
While the cake is baking, combine the lemon juice and icing sugar in a bowl. Set in a warm place so that the sugar dissolves in the juice.

Bring the hot cake from the oven and spoon the warm lemon syrup over the entire surface – the cake will soak it up.*

31

Leave until quite cold then, using the paper ends, lift the cake from the tin. Cut into squares.

The rind and juice of an orange could be used instead of the rind and juice of a lemon.

*Not quite true. The syrup tends to flow across the surface of the cake and down the sides, so that the centre gets very little or none of it. It is necessary to "hole" the cake all over.

OAT AND NUTTY BREAD
Blasé Roses

My mother's recipe. Makes one medium loaf.

300g/10 oz strong plain flour, sieved
115g/4 oz plain wholemeal flour
100g/3-1/2oz porridge oats
1 tsp salt

25g/1 oz unsalted butter
3/4 sachet easy-blend yeast
2 tbsp runny honey
55g/2 oz chopped nuts
325g warm milk (or half milk, half water)

For the topping
Milk to glaze
1 tbsp porridge oats
25g/1 oz chopped nuts

Place the flour, oats and salt in a large bowl. Rub in the butter until the mixture resembles fine breadcrumbs. Add the yeast, honey and nuts and stir well. Add the liquid and stir until a soft dough forms – you may need to add a little extra warm water.

Turn onto a lightly floured surface and knead for about 10 mins until smooth.

Shape into a round ball and place in an oiled bowl. Cover with oiled polythene and leave to rise in a warm place until double in size.

Turn the dough out and knock it down. Knead it until smooth and firm. Place in a 900g loaf tin, or shape as desired and place onto a baking sheet.

Cover with oiled polythene and leave in a warm place for about 30 mins, until doubled in size.

Preheat oven to 200°C/180°F/Gas Mark 6. Brush with milk and sprinkle over the extra oats and nuts. Bake in the preheated oven for 30-40 mins until risen and golden. Serve with unsalted butter.

SOUPS, SALADS AND PICKLES

CARROT SALAD
Julia Neuberger

2 lb carrots (or more)

1 tbsp granulated sugar, but may need more to taste

1 tsp salt
Wine vinegar (to taste)
6 oz raisins or sultanas
Large bunch fresh coriander

1 oz panch pooran (Indian 5-spice mix from any good Indian store)

1 tbsp olive oil

Toast the panch pooran in a pan without oil until the mustard seeds start popping.

Peel and grate the carrots.

Put in a large bowl and add raisins/sultanas, most of the coriander chopped, panch pooran, sugar and salt. Pour over wine vinegar and oil. Toss, taste, adjust seasonings.

Serve with chopped coriander on top for decoration.

Tastes even better on Day 2, but pour off juices before serving.

OVERNIGHT CUCUMBER PICKLE
Deborah Mendez

1 cucumber (400gm/12 oz)
1 onion (200gm/6 oz)
1 green pepper
1 tbsp salt

200ml/6fl. oz white vinegar
50g/2 oz white sugar
10g/1/2 oz celery seed

(All weights are approximate.)

Wash the cucumber. Do not peel. De-seed the green pepper.

Cut the cucumber, green pepper and onion into thin slices and put into a container. Stir the salt into the mixture, cover and leave in the refrigerator overnight.

Drain well and rinse with cold water to remove the salt. Pat dry. Mix the sugar, celery seeds and vinegar and pour over the vegetables.

Keep in the refrigerator in a closed container. This pickle will keep in the refrigerator for two to three months.

Adapt this recipe to your own taste – e.g. add sliced tomatoes instead of the green pepper. I used a red onion which gives the whole thing a pink colour.

MIXED BEAN SALAD
WITH CHILLI DRESSING
Anon

175g/6 oz canned red kidney beans, drained and rinsed

115g/4 oz canned sweetcorn, drained
1 red pepper, de-seeded and chopped

For the dressing
175ml/6fl. oz sunflower oil
4 x 15ml tbsp light soy sauce
4 x 15ml tbsp lemon juice
1 clove of garlic, peeled and crushed
1 green chilli, de-seeded and chopped
Freshly ground black pepper

For the topping
2 x 15ml tbsp fresh parsley, chopped

Mix all the vegetables together in a bowl. Put all the dressing ingredients into a glass screw-top jar, shake vigorously and add to the salad. Serve sprinkled with the parsley.

Serves four.

RED SALAD
Julia Wendon

6 cooked beetroot (ordinary supermarket kind in a plastic packet)

1 red onion
1 sweet red pepper
1 packet small plum tomatoes

1 crisp apple (optional)
1-2 pomegranates
Handful of flat-leaf parsley

For the dressing
Wine vinegar
Olive oil
1 tbsp pomegranate syrup
Salt and pepper

Dice beetroot and put in bowl. Dice onion and pepper and add. Cut tomatoes in half and add. Mix all together. (Depending on my mood, I will sometimes add a diced crisp apple.)

Cut the pomegranates in half across the "equator". Holding them carefully, bash their skin hard with a wooden spoon. All the glorious pink seeds come out leaving the yellow pith behind – satisfying and great for anger management! Add the seeds and mix. Chop the parsley and mix through.

Make the dressing
Combine one-third wine vinegar, two-thirds olive oil, a tablespoon of pomegranate syrup, salt and pepper. Mix to emulsify before dressing the salad.

Sometimes I will crumble on some feta cheese or goat's cheese to make a meal of it as opposed to something to eat with cold or warm chicken.

RUSSIAN SALAD
Blasé Roses

1 kg potatoes
5 carrots
1/2 lb peas (petits pois) frozen
4 tins tuna in oil, good quality
6 large eggs (for boiling)
200g green pitted olives
1 tin of roasted red peppers – use only 2 large ones for decoration

For the mayonnaise
6 eggs
Oil accordingly, good quality
1 lemon

Separately boil the potatoes, carrots, peas and eggs, then leave to cool down. Put them in the fridge for about one hour and they are easy to cut in small squares.

Drain oil from tuna fish, drain brine from olives and peppers. Make the mayonnaise and mix everything together in a large bowl. Leave overnight in the fridge.

The following day put in an oblong platter and decorate the top: first with a little mayonnaise to look good, then with boiled eggs, each one cut lengthways in four pieces, plus the rest of the olives and cut peppers in long thin pieces to give a good presentation.

Make the mayonnaise
The mayonnaise is very simple to make: beat 6 egg yolks only with a hand whisk, then add the oil a little at a time until you make the quantity needed. When finished, add the juice of 1 lemon and a pinch of salt and it is ready to use.

WIDELY LOVED PEA SOUP
Regina

Quite simple, will satisfy (many) hungry guests.

800g-900g peas (fresh or frozen)
1 Gem lettuce
125g butter (unsalted if possible)
1 litre water

Sugar
Salt
Pepper
Parsley
Yoghurt (or crème fraiche)

Melt butter in a large pan.

Cut Gem lettuce into narrow strips, add to the melted butter. Add 1 tsp sugar, salt and pepper to taste.

Stir well until lettuce is softened.

Add peas, cook gently for 10 min until peas are soaked and softened.

Add water and cook at moderate heat until peas are tender.

Purée the soup (in a food mixer or blender).

Serve hot, adding 1 tbsp of yoghurt (or crème fraiche) and some parsley to each bowl.

Delicious with a slice or two of toasted bread.

MAIN DISHES

CHEESE SOUFFLE
Julia Wendon

15g/1/2 oz butter
15g/1/2 oz flour
300ml milk
85g/3 oz strong grated Cheddar cheese

French mustard (optional)
3 eggs
Grated Parmesan cheese

Make a basic white sauce with the butter, flour and milk, in this way: melt the butter, then add the flour. Stir over a low heat to allow the flour to cook. Add the warmed milk bit by bit – slowly and stirring well after each addition to get rid of any lumps and ensure the flour has cooked.

Lightly butter a soufflé dish. Add the cheese to the white sauce, and some French mustard if desired. Stir until the cheese is melted. Let the sauce cool.

Separate the eggs. Once the sauce is cool, stir in the egg yolks. Chill the egg whites and then whisk until stiff (until the bowl can be safely turned upside-down above your head!).

Preheat the oven to 200°C. Fold the egg white into the sauce mixture, keeping all the air in the egg whites. The mixture should not come higher than three-quarters of the way up the soufflé dish.

Sprinkle some finely grated Parmesan cheese on top. Put in the oven and turn the temperature down to 180°C.

Cooking usually takes about 30 mins, and then it will all be gloriously brown and risen with crispy edges and a soft middle.

Serve with a jacket potato and butter, and lettuce with a French dressing.

CHICKEN HOMER (WITH SPINACH RICE)
Sophie Jhirad

This is my take on Chicken Gabriel, in which the honey etc is put into the cavity of the whole chicken, which goes into a special pot for roasting. An attempt to roast it without that pot resulted in failure. The name is derived from the ingredients, the R being the Rice that accompanies this dish (see recipe).

6-8 chicken thighs, weighing approx. 1-1/2 lb
2 dessertspoons honey
2 onions, halved and sliced, slices broken up
1/2 cup Marsala (Madeira if you feel extravagant)
1-2 tbsp mixed herbs
Salt and pepper to taste

Use a saucepan that will take the chicken pieces in one layer. Put the wine and honey on to heat. Add the salt, pepper and mixed herbs. When the liquid starts simmering, give it a good stir to make sure the honey is completely dissolved.

As soon as it begins to boil, put in the chicken, skin-side up. In a couple of minutes, turn the pieces over. Cover the pan and leave to cook over medium heat (the liquid should be simmering briskly, *not* boiling, or the chicken will not get a chance to take in the flavours).

Add the onion when the chicken is half-cooked
(10-15 mins). Don't worry if it will not all fit into the liquid. Both chicken and onion will be adding their juices, and it does no harm for some of the onion to cook in the steam. After a while, stir the softened onion into the liquid. If liked, give the chicken another turn during cooking.

Should not take more than three-quarters of an hour (I've known it to take 20 mins).

CHICKEN PILAF IN A LEMON SAUCE
Julia Wendon

1 chicken
Carrots
Onion
Peppercorns

Bay leaf
Rice
Lemon juice

Put a large boiling chicken/fowl in water with carrots, onion, peppercorns and salt as appropriate, and a bay leaf if desired. When stock and chicken are cooked (approx. 3 hours), strain the stock and keep.

Place the chicken on a plate and joint it. Put the large pieces to one side, and put the smaller bits of meat and shreds you pull off the bones onto another plate.

Fry an onion until soft in chicken fat (or oil). Add rice and stir until translucent. Add stock in a ratio of 1:2.5 (one cup of rice to 2-1/2 cups of liquid), then add the small pieces of chicken left over from jointing.

Cover and cook over a low heat until the rice absorbs all the stock. Keep the lid on the saucepan and keep warm.

For the sauce
In a separate saucepan take the reminder of the drained stock, warm it through and add some lemon juice to flavour. (Check seasoning. Some of the family add some saffron at this point, but I don't.) Add about 2 egg yolks and warm to allow sauce to thicken – do not boil.

Put the dish together by spooning the rice onto a serving plate, and placing the warm chicken joints on top. We usually spoon the sauce over the chicken and rice and serve – however, you could serve all the components separately and allow people to help themselves to the sauce. Feeds about four people.

For pudding we usually had either black fruit compote or stewed apples.

FISH CAKES
Blasé Roses

My mother's recipe.

1-1/2 lb haddock fillets, skinned and boned
1 onion, peeled
1 potato, peeled
1-1/2 tsp sea salt

1/4 tsp white pepper
9 heaped tbsp fine matzo meal
2 tbsp oil
2 large eggs, beaten
Oil for deep frying

Chop haddock finely in a food processor, and transfer to a bowl. Then put the onion and potato through the processor.

Strain the chopped onion and potato and add to the fish (reserving the juice).

Add the salt, pepper, 4 tbsp of the matzo meal and oil.

Gently mix everything together with the eggs and the reserved juice.

If the mixture seems a bit dry, leave to rest for an hour or so in the fridge.

Wet hands and form the mixture into fish cakes. Dredge over the rest of the matzo meal.

Deep fry in oil for about 7-8 mins turning gently. Drain oil.

FISH STEW
Blasé Roses

My mother's recipe. Serves 4, cooking time 40 mins.

1 tbsp olive oil
2 onions, chopped
4 sticks celery, chopped
4 large cloves garlic, chopped

400g chopped tomatoes, fresh or canned
500g potatoes, peeled and cut into 3cm-4cm chunks
2-3 bay leaves
500ml vegetable stock

Black pepper
600g fish fillets (salmon, cod or tilapia)
Juice of one small lemon
15g fresh flat-leaf parsley, chopped

15g fresh dill, chopped
1-2 tbsp capers (optional)

Heat the olive oil in a saucepan, and fry the onions and celery for about 5 mins. Add the garlic and continue to cook for 3-4 mins.

Add the tomatoes, potatoes, bay leaves and stock, and season with black pepper. Bring to the boil, lower heat and simmer for 15 mins.

Add the fish and simmer for a further 10-15 mins until potatoes are tender and fish is cooked. Add the lemon juice, herbs and capers (if using).

Check the seasoning and serve with slices of Oat and Nutty Bread (see recipe) spread with unsalted butter.

FRICASSEE
Julia Wendon

Previously this was done with diced veal but, given some people's sensitivities, it could also be made with diced turkey breast.

1-2 onions
2 cloves garlic
Veal or turkey breast
Mushrooms
White wine sauerkraut (bought)
Oil for frying

Chop onions finely. Lightly fry with a couple of cloves of garlic until soft. Set aside.

Dice meat if not already done. Fry and lightly brown the meat in some oil in a deep frying-pan. Add the onions and garlic.

Season with salt, pepper and Italian herbs/seasoning (oregano, basil). Thinly slice mushrooms, and add.

Add a little water, and cover and cook until the meat is tender. Just before serving, thicken with some soya cream and grainy mustard.

Serve with some white wine sauerkraut. (I have to be honest here: I buy it by the jar these days but have memories of it being made at home.)

HOT AND SPICY CHICKEN
Blasé Roses

My grandmother's recipe. Serves 4 people.

4 whole legs of chicken
3 mixed peppers (red and green)
3 large onions
2 cups of peas (petits pois) frozen

1 cup of dry white wine
4 cloves of garlic
2 tbsp fresh chopped parsley
4 tsp cumin powder

4 tsp paprika
Chilli powder according to taste
Salt according to taste
1/4 cup oil

3 tins chopped tomatoes
Rice

Preheat oven to 180°C/350°F/Gas Mark 4.

Wash chicken well and drain.

Put chicken in an oven tray and add cumin powder, paprika, chilli and salt.

Chop onions, garlic, peppers and parsley, and mix with chicken.

Add the tomatoes, oil and white wine. Mix together and put in preheated oven for about one hour – check when it is cooked by inserting a skewer or knife.

Serve with cooked rice (long-grain American brown rice).

LAMB SHANKS
Pam Millard

I asked my son which of my recipes he especially liked and associated with "Mum's cooking". He gave me two: stewed apples, and this one for lamb shanks.

1 lamb shank per person
Big pinch of dried or fresh mint
2 tsp tomato paste
2 carrots, peeled and cut in large chunks

Stick of celery, halved
Courgette if you have one
Black pepper
Vegetable stock cubes (see how many below)
1 glass red wine (optional)

Take fat off lamb shanks and rinse under running cold water. Place shanks in an oven-proof lidded casserole large enough for each shank to sit on the bottom.

Pour in sufficient water (could include a little red wine) to nearly cover the shanks, and add the appropriate number of stock cubes. (One or two, depending on the size of the casserole.) Put in the rest of the ingredients.

Cover and cook in the oven on 180°C/356°F/Gas Mark 4 for 1-1/2 hours. It can cook on the hob, but you need to keep more of an eye on the liquid in case it dries up too much. Cook till the meat can be pulled apart with a fork. It is hard to overcook this dish.

It tastes delicious reheated so it can be prepared a few hours before serving. If reheating from cold, take the fat off the top of the liquid before reheating.

Serve with rice and green beans, and maybe some red cabbage – pour over as much of the liquid as your diners fancy.

I often turn the left-over liquid into a soup or stock for risotto.

MUSHROOM PILAF
Julia Wendon

Mushrooms
Stock
Long-grain rice

Make chicken stock (in the old-fashioned way by boiling a chicken carcass with carrots and onions), or if for a milchy (milchedik) meal, use vegetable stock.

Take a mixture of mushrooms (good flavour as per your choice) and fry in chicken fat or oil.

Add rice (long grain) to the mushrooms and stir though until translucent for a few minutes only.

Add stock to rice and mushrooms at a ratio of 1:2.5 (one cup of rice to 2-1/2 cups of liquid).

Put lid on saucepan and simmer on a low heat until all stock is absorbed.

Serve with a green salad and a French dressing (oil, vinegar and Dijon mustard).

SMOKED SALMON AND COTTAGE CHEESE TORTE
Issy Benjamin

After a study session on highly spiritual matters or a deep meditation, it is customary to have what is known as a *siyum* – a communal celebratory meal intended to "ground" the participants, to bring them back to earth, to the reality of this mundane existence.

At one such *siyum* I found myself re-transported to the upper realm of bliss as I tasted the offering of one of the participants – a ravishing dancing teacher. It was a matching confection in the shape of a wedge of melt-in-your-mouth layered torte composed of alternating layers of smoked salmon and cottage cheese interleaved between slightly sweet pancakes.

I was totally smitten – but "spoken for" at the time – so I merely asked her for the recipe, which she gladly shared. It was a labour of love, which involved preparing a smooth pancake mix and frying six thin pancakes – between which, when cool, the smoked salmon and cottage cheese were interleaved.

I acknowledged the time and trouble she had devoted to preparing this heavenly dish, but put it "on the back burner" as it involved so much effort – until the day I found, in a local supermarket, packs of readymade pancakes.

At that stage of my life I was perforce once more back in a bachelor state, with a male philosophy of catering – if it took longer than ten minutes to prepare, it was not worth doing!

And suddenly, unexpectedly, here within my grasp was a heavenly dish which could fulfill that criterion – and I gladly share the recipe.

6 ready-made sweet pancakes

500g long-slice smoked salmon (I
in emergency I have used the same quantity of cheaper "salmon pieces" – off-cuts
from the slicing process.)

Approx. 900g natural cottage cheese (6% fat)

49

Place a pancake on a suitably sized dinner plate.

Cover the entire pancake with a thin layer of smoked salmon, on top of which spread a thin layer of cottage cheese, sufficient to *just* cover the entire surface of the smoked salmon. (Thicker to taste if you are a lover of cottage cheese – experimentation will eventually give you the best proportions.)

Place the next pancake over to cover, pressing down firmly. Repeat four more times to form a five-layer torte.

Place an inverted dinner plate over the torte and press down to consolidate. Trim away excess squeezings of salmon and cottage cheese to form a neat round torte.

Serve cold – cut into 16 elegant wedges.

SPANISH OMELETTE (TORTILLA)
Blasé Roses

7 potatoes, weight about 1-1⁄4 kilo
1 large onion
6 large eggs
3 cups olive oil
Salt to taste

Cut the (raw) potatoes thinly, like crisps. Slice the onion.

Mix the potatoes and onion together. Add salt to taste and fry until they are soft and a little brown, turning often so they don't get burned.

When ready, put them in a colander to drain the oil out.

Crack the eggs into a large mixing bowl and whisk well. Then add the potato and onion mixture with a large spoon.

Pour 1 tsp olive oil into a 9in-10in frying pan and heat on a medium heat. Be careful not to get the pan too hot, because the oil will burn – or the tortilla will.

Add the mixture, spreading evenly to allow the eggs to cook around the edges.

Carefully turn the tortilla by putting a plate on top of the frying pan and turning it upside down. Now slip the tortilla back into the frying pan. Do this two or three times – it depends how well the mixture is cooked. When finished, let the tortilla cool for 2 mins.

VEGETABLES

BLACK-EYED BEANS
Sophie Jhirad

While not restricted to the Sabbath, black-eyed beans used to be cooked by the Bené Israel for the Sabbath afternoon, started off on Friday before the Sabbath began and left to cook overnight ready for Saturday lunch. The recipe given here is not the one then used.

10-12 oz black-eyed beans
2 onions, sliced
3 tbsp vegetable oil
Salt
2 well-rounded dessertspoons concentrated tomato purée

1 tsp good curry powder (more to taste)
OR
1 tsp each chilli powder, ground ginger, garlic powder, ground coriander

Wash beans, cover generously with cold water, and leave to soak for at least 6 hours, overnight if wanted for lunch.

On medium heat, cook onions in the oil, stirring now and then until soft. Do not brown. While the sliced onion is cooking, drain the beans and wash in repeated rinses of cold water until the water runs clear.

Add curry powder (or the alternative) to cooked onion and stir well in. Cook, stirring, for a few seconds. Add the beans and mix well with the onion and spices. Cover and leave to cook, stirring occasionally (add a tablespoon or two of *hot* water if necessary), until the beans are no longer raw and a fork can be just pushed through one.

Add hot water to cover the beans, bring to a good boil, lower temperature to simmering, cover, and leave to cook, giving the beans a good stir every 5 to 7 mins to make sure nothing's sticking to the bottom of the pan.

When the beans are cooked, add salt to taste, and finally the tomato purée – more if you want a thicker sauce, in which case check if more salt is needed.

Note: Coconut rice (see recipe) goes well with this dish. If you wish to avoid cooking both dishes at the same time, fine-grated carrot is an excellent alternative.

CABBAGE AND CARAWAY SEEDS
Julia Wendon

1 white cabbage
Oil or butter
Water
Caraway seed

Chop cabbage reasonably finely (3mm).

Warm some oil or butter in a saucepan. Place in the cabbage and stir around.

Put in a drop or two of water and put the lid on and cook for about 3 mins.

Add the caraway seed, amount to taste (1-3 tsp).

Put back on heat without the saucepan lid and allow the water to evaporate and the cabbage to be cooked *al dente* (not too soft).

COCONUT RICE
Norah Solomon

1 cup rice
1-1/2 cups water*
2 whole cardamoms
1/4 tsp turmeric

1 inch from a tablet of creamed coconut (a tablet is 198g/7 oz)

Salt

Wash rice and wash cardamoms. Put water, creamed coconut, cardamom, turmeric and salt into a saucepan. Bring to the boil. Stir to check the coconut is completely dissolved.

Add rice, bring back to the boil, cover, reduce heat to just simmering. Leave to cook. When nearly all the water is absorbed, test a grain of rice. If still slightly raw, add just a little hot water. When rice is just cooked, reduce heat to absolute minimum for 3 mins before taking off the stove and serving.

*The usual ratio of rice to water is 1 to 2, but because of the coconut here, less water is needed.

FRUIT AND NUT PULAO
Sophie Jhirad

This, from *The Sainsbury Book of Casseroles*, works very well, particularly when a vegetarian friend comes to stay. I've made just one adjustment – re the rice. And one day, discovering I had no flaked almonds but, luckily, did have a packet of pine nuts, I used those instead. Serves 6.

75g/3 oz sultanas
175g/6 oz dried fruit (apricots, apples, pears etc)
1 tbsp sweet sherry
75g/3 oz butter
1 onion, finely chopped
1/4 pint/150ml measure of long-grain rice
Half a vegetable stock cube
1/2 teaspoon ground Allspice
Salt and pepper
50g/2 oz flaked almonds (or pine nuts)

Put the sultanas and dried fruit in a bowl, sprinkle with the sherry and cover with water. Leave to soak for four hours. Drain, and chop the apricots, apples, pears etc.

Cook the rice with the stock cube in double the quantity of water. Preheat the oven to 190°C/375°F/Gas Mark 5 (moderately hot).

Melt the butter in a frying pan, add the onion and fry until softened. Stir in the rice and Allspice, then add salt and pepper to taste and mix well.

Fold in the fruit and almonds, then turn the mixture into a greased casserole dish. Bake in the oven for 30 mins.

NB: Nervous of an overflow, I use a saucepan instead of a frying pan.

GREEN CHUTNEY (LIQUIDIZER METHOD)
Sophie Jhirad

In India, every kitchen is equipped with a large grinding stone. Between that and a smaller, specially shaped stone, hand-held, are ground fresh grated coconut, coriander and the other herbs with just enough water to make a thick paste. This is a savoury base for cooking meat or stuffing fish. To be used as a chutney, a teaspoon of sugar and a squeeze of lime or lemon juice are mixed in. Here, the (concentrated) creamed coconut is sweet enough and the vinegar renders the lemon juice unnecessary (it also lengthens the life of the chutney).

1 LARGE bunch fresh coriander
3 oz creamed coconut (comes in 198g/7 oz packets)
2-5 green chillies

1 tsp fresh root ginger, peeled, washed and chopped

2-6 cloves garlic, peeled and chopped
A few mint leaves (optional)
Salt
Vinegar and water

Prepare the chillies: wash, take off the stalk end, remove seeds by slitting down the centre, chop.

Scrape or chop the creamed coconut. Combine with the chillies, garlic, ginger, mint leaves and a little salt.

Wash the coriander after discarding the roots. You may find some tender little green bits at their base – save these. Take in the stems to the point where they become tough. Chop, taking care that nothing is long enough to wind round the blades of the liquidizer.

Place a third of the coriander in the liquidizer goblet, add half the coconut-herbs mixture, then the second third of the coriander, the rest of the coconut-herbs mixture, and finally the remaining coriander.

Gently pour in vinegar to a quarter the height of what is in the goblet; make up to a third with water. Liquidize until smooth, switching off once or twice to scrape down the sides and to check if the quantities of herbs and salt are to your taste, adding more if necessary. If too chilli-hot, add more coconut with a little more vinegar/water.

Pour into a bowl (ex-houmous pots make excellent containers). At this stage the chutney is a little runny, but in an hour or so will firm up. It will keep for a week in the fridge, freezes well and will then keep for a month.

Some people make this with desiccated coconut – turns out grainy in appearance as well as to taste.

Uses:

1. A sandwich filling – do not butter the bread.

2. An accompaniment to some meat and chicken dishes.

3. Mixed with yoghurt, a sauce to go with Green Pea Pulao (see recipe).

GREEN PEA PULAO
Sophie Jhirad

This is my mother's recipe – so satisfying that, with the green chutney sauce (see recipe), we needed no extra addition to the meal. My only contribution is to suggest alternatives to three of the ingredients.

1/4 kilo rice

1/2 kilo green peas (before shelling) or 300g frozen green peas

Milk of one coconut or 1/4 slab of creamed coconut, dissolved in 380ml water

1 tbsp ghee* or butter
2 in cinnamon stick
5-6 cloves
2 medium-sized onions, sliced fine
Salt

Cashew nuts and/or almonds (blanched), sliced and toasted (optional)

Khus-khus (poppy seeds), washed, dried and toasted (optional)

Heat ghee to boiling, add cinnamon and cloves. After 2 mins, add the onion. Cook until the onion browns. Take out half, put on a warm plate and leave in a warm place.

Add rice to what is in the saucepan, mix well. After 5 mins, add the green peas, mix well. Add the coconut milk and salt, stir in well. Bring to the boil, then reduce heat to a simmer. Cover and leave to cook.

Best when fresh and hot. When serving, sprinkle with the reserved onion and with the (optional) nuts and khus-khus.

Accompaniment: Green Chutney mixed with yoghurt to form a thick sauce.

*Ghee is clarified butter. If you substitute butter for the ghee, use a bit more than a tablespoon. Be careful, as butter burns more easily than ghee.

RED CABBAGE
Julia Wendon

1 red cabbage
Chicken fat or oil
1-2 dessertspoons sugar
Wine vinegar
Water

Take a red cabbage and chop finely. Some like it finer, some coarser. I'm a midway person, with slices being about 2-3mm. Hey, it's a cabbage – relax.

Take a heavy-duty saucepan and heat a little fat (chicken fat or oil). Add the cabbage. On a low heat, stir it around so it softens and doesn't burn.

Add a dessertspoon of sugar (more if preferred), and then a tablespoon of wine vinegar. Season to taste. Add a slurp or two of water so things don't burn.

Put a close-fitting lid on the saucepan and cook for about 1-1/2 to 2 hours on a low heat on top of the stove (or same time in the oven at 150°C (2 hours).

When cooked, set aside for at least 24 hours and then rewarm and enjoy with goose/duck breasts or any other meat dish. Or if you are like me, just eat it by the plateful as a meal alongside white cabbage with caraway seeds.

SPINACH RICE
Sophie Jhirad

1/4 pint measure of long-grain rice
1/2 vegetable stock cube, or salt to taste
3-4 chunks of frozen finely chopped spinach

Put the rice and stock cube (or salt) into a saucepan with double the quantity of water. Bring to the boil, covered. Check that the stock cube has dissolved and stir it in with a fork, carefully. (Respect the diktat that rice should not be stirred, but do not be a slave to it.)

Add the spinach chunks, pushing them gently into the rice. Bring back to the boil, cover and reduce heat to a simmer. After 5 mins, stir the by-now dissolved spinach into the rice, cover and continue to simmer until done. This, altogether, should not take more than 20 mins.

NB: Spinach is anathema to some people, but I know someone who, after declaring a dislike, ate this quite happily – to her surprise!

STUFFED AUBERGINE
Blasé Roses

My grandmother's recipe.

2 large aubergines
4 tbsp olive oil
2 medium onions, finely chopped
12 black olives in brine or vinegar

2 handfuls of drained capers
2 handfuls of parmesan cheese
4-6 garlic cloves, finely chopped
2 handfuls of fresh white breadcrumbs

Parsley, chives, basil, pepper, salt
4 anchovies (optional)
1 tin chopped tomatoes
Salt for preparation

Cut the aubergine in half lengthways. With a sharp knife, make horizontal and vertical slashes through the flesh in a crisscross pattern, being careful not to pierce the skin. Work in lots of salt to draw out any bitterness.

Set aside for 30 mins, then rinse the aubergines and pat dry. Scoop out the squares. Heat the oil in a frying pan and fry the aubergine skins gently until golden brown. Remove from the pan and place on a baking tray. Gently fry the onions until soft. Then add the aubergine squares for a few minutes until they break down.

Remove from the heat and mix the rest of the ingredients (including the anchovies if using), and a few tablespoons of brine or vinegar from the olives. Spoon this mixture into the aubergine skins, pressing down the filling. Bake for about 20 mins until the stuffing is crisp on top.

SWEETS AND DESSERTS

TIPS

CHOCOLATE

In cooking, it is unnecessary – and possibly unwise – to use dark chocolate with the highest percentage of cocoa. Between 50 and 60 percent is fine. But check the ingredients – not long ago there was on the market a dark chocolate that contained butter from cow's milk, withdrawn since then, we hope. Adding extra butter means the truffles won't work! (See Chocolate Almond Truffles recipe.)

CINNAMON

There are two kinds of cinnamon. The superior is True Cinnamon: the dried inner bark of the tree is the spice. It comes in fine curls, rolled to form "sticks", and is very brittle. The other is Cassia Cinnamon: the bark of the tree comprises the spice. It comes in pieces, dark brown on the outside and paler on the inside. It is of course cheaper than true cinnamon, but has very much the same smell and taste.

CARAMELISED ORANGES
Julia Wendon

6 large oranges
75ml water
100g sugar

Peel the oranges with a sharp knife, removing all the white pith.

Put them in a relatively shallow bowl which you'll be using as the serving dish (this way you will catch all the nice orange juice).

Take an orange and lay it on a chopping board with its central axis lying horizontal and cut slices from one end to the other – they should be 3-5mm thick. Repeat with the rest of the oranges.

Lay out the sliced oranges in the serving dish.

For the caramel
Put the water and sugar in a pan over a low heat.

Heat gently and allow to boil gently until you can see a change in colour to gold and "smell" the caramel forming.

Take the caramel off the heat and pour over the oranges.

It will go wonderfully hard and also create a lovely juice that mixes with the orange juice. Ideally, serve in the next few hours.

Do warn your guests about the risks of damage to dental fillings from eating caramel!!!

CARROT HALVA
Sophie Jhirad

A halva is any sweet that sets (blancmange is a kind of halva) or that is spooned, like this one.

1 lb carrots, peeled and fine grated
1 pint full-cream milk
Pinch of salt
Sugar to taste
1 tsp butter
Ground cardamom to taste

Almonds and/or pistachios, blanched and chopped or finely slivered (optional)

Place carrots, milk and salt in a wide saucepan or deep frying-pan, and bring to the boil. Reduce heat, and let simmer, *uncovered.* At this stage, unless the level of the contents is dangerously near the top of the pan, there is no need to stand over it, stirring. You can carry out some little task and come back every few minutes to give the mixture a stir. As the milk is absorbed and reduced, you will need to scrape down the sides of the pan.

When the milk is reduced to less than half, stir every few seconds and then continually to prevent the halva burning. Add the sugar when the liquid is almost absorbed: begin with 1 dessertspoon, taste, and add more as required. When the sugar is quite absorbed, add the butter. Cook, stirring, until, when you press the back of a spoon into the halva, *no* liquid seeps into the bowl. Then add the cardamom and stir well in.

Take off the heat and leave to cool, stirring occasionally to prevent a skin forming. The nuts can be mixed into the cooling halva or sprinkled over after it has been turned out into a dish.

NB:

1. The carrot/milk proportion can be varied – I know someone who puts 1 lb carrot, coarse-grated, into 2 pints milk.

2. To double the quantity, but save space and time, use 1 pint milk and 1/2 pint cream to 2 lb carrots.

3. If you feel extravagant, drape a sheet of silver leaf over the cooled halva – yes, it can be safely eaten.

CHOCOLATE ALMOND TRUFFLES
Sophie Jhirad

Way back in Bombay my father used to get the Daily Mirror, a week's issues bound in yellow newsprint covered with ads. There would be a pageful of cartoon strips – funny, serious, practical – and at the foot of the page a recipe. I cut them out and still have the lot, but must confess this is the only one I've ever tried. Oddly, it called for a whole egg – fatal to the first try-out. To match the two egg yolks of the Chocolate Coffee Truffles, I've doubled the quantities given in the original recipe. This quantity makes 60 to 65 truffles. They can last for a long time.

12 oz icing sugar
8 oz ground almonds
4 oz cocoa
Whites of two large eggs, lightly beaten
Icing sugar to coat

Make ready a tray lined with foil. The ingredients can be put together by hand, but a mixer does save time and effort. I use the K beater of the Kenwood.

Sieve the icing sugar and cocoa into a bowl. Add the ground almonds, cutting in gently with a spatula to prevent the dry ingredients flying. Add the egg-white and bring all together – if using a mixer, at the lowest speed. Form into a large lump. Break off pieces to roll into little balls, flattening each slightly.

Do not coat the truffles at this stage, as they will just absorb the icing sugar and you will have to do it all over again – apart from making them sweeter! As you form each truffle, dab it in the icing sugar just enough to prevent it sticking to the foil, and lay it on the tray. An hour or two should be enough to then finish off by rolling the truffles in the icing sugar.

Note: If you find after the addition of the egg white, the stuff won't stick together but is too dry, add a little hot water.

CHOCOLATE COFFEE TRUFFLES
Sophie Jhirad

This recipe began life years ago in the pages of Homes and Gardens as Chocolate Rum Truffles. The substitution of coffee makes it less sweet – and easier to form the truffles. This quantity makes 35-45 truffles.

6 oz dark chocolate
3 dessertspoons single cream
1-1/2 oz butter
2 egg yolks
7 oz icing sugar, sieved

2-3 dessertspoons instant coffee, dissolved in 2-3 dessertspoons of water

Chocolate powder to coat

Put chocolate and coffee in a heatproof bowl and set over hot water for the chocolate to melt. Beat in the butter and then the cream, making sure each is thoroughly mixed in before adding the next. Strain the egg yolk into the bowl (this is the tricky bit, but you don't want the yolk-skin gumming up the works). Beat this in well, then add the icing sugar.

Leave to cool, stirring now and then to prevent a skin forming. At this stage the mixture is too soft to work. Give it a while to firm up, and in the meantime make ready a tray lined with foil.

Form into little balls, flatten slightly. Do not coat them yet, as they will absorb the chocolate powder and you will have to do it all over again. Dip each truffle to pick up just enough chocolate powder to prevent it sticking to the foil, and put it on the tray to dry out. An hour or two should be enough to then finish off by rolling the truffles in the chocolate powder.

Warning: Do not sit in a warm place while forming these truffles and do not leave them in a warm place, or they will go all soft and squidgy!

GOOSEBERRY KUCHEN
Julia Wendon

For the pastry
125g flour
50g caster sugar
2 egg yolks
2 oz butter
Pinch salt

For pesachdik pastry
5 oz butter
3 oz caster sugar
1 egg
4 oz potato flour
4 oz fine cake meal (matzo)

For the frangipane
1 egg yolk
1 egg
100g caster sugar
100g ground almonds
2 level tbsp flour or potato flour
Cream
Butter
Raspberry jam

For the meringue
2 egg whites
120g caster sugar
1/4 tsp cream of tartar

Gooseberries

Make short-crust pastry, line a square baking tin with it and bake blind. (During Pesach this was a pesachdik pastry.)

Make the frangipane
Combine cream and butter. Beat in sugar until light and fluffy. Gradually add eggs, beating after each addition. Stir in the ground almonds and flour (or

potato flour). Put in the pastry case. Dot the top with good-quality raspberry jam.

Make the meringue
Take 2 egg whites and beat until they form soft peaks. Fold in 60g caster sugar and continue to beat until glossy. Fold in the next 60g of caster sugar and the cream of tartar with a metal spoon. Pour or place on top of the frangipane.

Add the gooseberries
The other way I remember as a child is that Mum used to stew fresh gooseberries (with a little water and sugar). When the fruit was still just holding together, she'd take it off the heat and cool it. The gooseberries were then drained, and the whole fruits dropped into the egg-white mixture.

The best bit then as children was that we were allowed to drink the gooseberry juices when they had cooled, in a glass. The memory is still quite delicious!! Or as I got older the gooseberry juices were used on cornflakes rather than milk – I've always had rather strange tastes!!

Take the kuchen and cook at 180°C for about 30 mins. Serve as a pudding or with a cup of black tea.

ROTE GRUETZE
Julia Wendon

Red fruits (raspberries, redcurrants, blackcurrants)

Sugar to taste
Arrowroot
Cream or ice cream and biscuits to accompany

Stew the fruits with sugar.

Strain through muslin – or nowadays through a fine sieve or "mouli". Add a little arrowroot to thicken.

Serve cold with cream or ice cream and a suitable fine biscuit (thin and crispy).

SPICY APPLES
Sophie Jhirad

Up to 8 Bramley apples
1 lb cube sugar
1-2 lemons
Cinnamon sticks (at least 7in)

Day One
Cut the zest from the lemon(s) and put with the cinnamon into a quarter pint of water. Bring just to the boil, take off the stove and leave in a warm place.

Day Two
Peel and core the apples.

Strain the liquid into the saucepan you are going to use, squeeze the lemons, add the juice and stir. Add the sugar cubes, put on the gentlest heat, and when the sugar has completely dissolved, bring to the boil.

Put in the apples (there must be only one layer, so you may have to cook them in two batches). When the apples are in, you will find the liquid boils up very strongly, so that it can be difficult to see what is happening to them.

Turn the apples over very gently when they've been in for some time (use your judgement). Test with a fork and, when done, remove with a slotted spoon into a dish, not a plate.

Boil down the remaining liquid and pour over – boiling liquid is very deceptive, and when cold may turn out to be too thick, so again, use your judgement.

Serve with whipped cream.

STEWED APPLES
Pam Millard

This recipe varies according to what I have in the cupboard. How do I write a recipe like that? I'll have to be like my grandmother when I asked her how much flour went into her cake recipe. "Half a bowl," came the reply. "Yes, but how many ounces?" I doggedly asked. "You know my bowl!" was her exasperated response. So, just experiment with the taste you want. For 6 people.

4 large Bramley cooking apples peeled and cored, sliced or in chunks

Large handful of sultanas or raisins
6 dried apricots halved or quartered
Orange juice
Cinnamon to taste
Handful of pine nuts (optional)
Handful of buckwheat (if you want crunchy bits)

Put all the ingredients into a medium-sized saucepan or casserole.

Pour over enough orange juice to cover the base. More if you want the apples moist, less if you want them drier.

Cover and cook on the hob for 40 mins. Or cover and put in the oven for 40 mins on 180°C/356°F/Gas Mark 4.

Test the softness of the apples as they cook. Beware of over-cooking: it either bubbles up and over or sticks to the pan and burns!

Serve hot or cold with fruit purée, cream or ice cream. A few drops of Amaretto liqueur makes it more exciting.

TURINOIS
June Levy

This is my favourite recipe – it never fails and is always a winner. It is very rich, so a little goes a long way. I was working at the Association for the Advancement of Science in 1979 and a colleague called Elva gave me a collection of her favourite recipes.

439g/15-3/4 oz can unsweetened chestnut purée
4 oz caster sugar
4 oz unsalted butter
6 oz plain chocolate

Cream butter and sugar thoroughly.

Melt chocolate with about 2 tbsp water, and allow to cool a little. Then add to the creamed butter and sugar with the chestnut purée. Mix well.

Flavour to taste.

Lightly oil a loaf tin (or push-up base tin – 8in square is recommended) and cover the base with greaseproof paper (also oiled).

Turn out the mixture into the tin and smooth the top over. Cover with foil and put in the fridge till the next day. Serve masked with whipped cream.

Can be frozen and used later.

THE END

Printed in Great Britain
by Amazon